3-50

RICHMONI CENSUS (

Simon Fowler

Special Paper Number 1
RICHMOND LOCAL HISTORY SOCIETY

R I C H M O N D   I N   T H E   C E N S U S   O F   1 8 5 1

by

Simon Fowler

Census returns are a neglected source for the study of local history. They present however a picture of any Victorian town or village area in more detail than virtually any other other documentary source.

In this pamphlet I have tried to give a brief introduction to the census records for Richmond in 1851, through the provision of indexes to the streets and surnames, together with a statistical guide, and have tried to build up a picture of what the town was like at the time of the Census, sometimes with the help of other documents. Britain in 1851 was at the height of the industrial revolution, and of its influence worldwide. There were no grim mines and factories in Richmond, however, and remarkably few people seem to have experienced the industrial revolution at first hand. The biggest industry was probably house building. The town was a mixture of the old and the new. Within the parish boundaries lay farms, which within a few short years would disappear for ever. It is curious to read entries for agricultural labourers and cowmen in the returns.

The first expansion of suburban growth was just beginning, but as yet was confined to commuters who could afford the high railway fares. Richmond was an exceptionally prosperous place. The economic life of the town centred around satisfying the needs of a relatively large upper and middle class. There was of course some poverty around, probably much less than in areas of comparative size at the time, and the study looks in some detail at these people who are so often neglected in the many books on Richmond.

These returns are available for public inspection either in the Public Record Office Census Room, Portugal Street, London WC2 or the Richmond Reference Library, Old Town Hall, Whittaker Avenue, Richmond, Surrey. The Public Record Office reference for these returns is HO 107/1605 folios 1-338.

The pamphlet is in several parts. The first three sections are: a general overview of Richmond in 1851; a statistical analysis of three Enumeration Districts; and a list of two hundred interesting or important entries in the Returns. The fourth part is a street index to the census returns; the fifth part is an index, arranged in surname order, of everybody resident in Richmond on census night 30 March 1851.

Throughout the introductory section references to individuals in the Census Returns have the following notation following their name (fnn). This refers to the folio where they may be found in the Returns.

< 1 >

R i c h m o n d   i n   1 8 5 1

It is difficult to imagine the town of Richmond as it was one hundred and thirty and five years ago in 1851. Accounts do exist, either in one of the guide books which extolled the pleasures of Richmond, or in the few surviving written memories of the people who lived there at the time. There are early photographs, showing the citizens of the town standing stiffly in dusty streets.

Guide books were keen, then as now, to describe the view from Richmond Hill, the pleasures of the Star and Garter Hotel, or the attractions of the village.

Thus theRailway Excursionist's Handbook to Richmond, Kew and Hampton Court (1) for example commented
> What need is there to travel up the Rhine however
> fashionable it may be - compelled to submit to
> ruinous extortion, to drink sour wine, to inhale
> perpetual tobacco smoke, and to sleep on hard beds
> with the combined horrors of dirt and "industrious
> fleas" - what need, we say, to count all these
> discomforts, when half an hours ride on the South
> Western Railway will bring the sight seeker to
> such a scene as Richmond and the pleasure seeker
> to such a hostelry as the Star and Garter.

A few years later a guide to Kew, Richmond, Twickenham and Hampton Court (2) could describe Richmond
> Though somewhat irregular, the village of Richmond
> is substantially built. It consists of several
> main streets, the most important being George
> Street, King Street and Hill Street. It is well
> lit and paved. Many of the shops are of a very
> superior description and exhibit in abundance
> every object and article or demand among a wealthy
> and always large population. The great influx of
> visitors to which it is liable may be readily
> inferred from the numbers of inns and hotels of
> all sizes and pretensions. There is nothing
> marked in the character of the street
> architecture; but numerous villas have of late
> years been rising in the outskirts giving an air
> if wealth and luxury to the place. The population
> consists to a considerable extent, of individuals
> of comfortable independencies, who have been
> attracted thither by the beauty of the scenery,
> and the salubriousness of the climate, taken in
> connection with its conginuity to London. Many
> wealthy citizens of the metropolis guided by the
> same motives have also made this their place of
> residence.

There is only one description of the town in the 1850s, written by a resident who was there then. This was an article written by Sir Edward Hertslet in about 1892, the most distinguished of Foreign Office Librarians, who moved to Richmond in 1852 (3). In it he describes the rustic nature of Richmond in the early 1850s. He also comments upon the church:

< 2 >

It was not easy for a stranger in those days to
get a seat in the Parish Church. On Sundays for a
tip of one shilling to the Pew Opener only secured
him an indifferent seat. But if he, or she,
aspired to a seat in the old high pews - about
five feet high and lined with green blaize or blue
serge - a tip of 2s 6d was expected, and I know
that it was not infrequently paid.

And the tollgate upon Richmond Bridge
Toll gates then stood at the foot of Richmond
Bridge and a charge of ½d was made for every foot
passenger

Early Victorian Richmond does not seem to be a period which
has attracted later historians, perhaps because the town had
ceased to be fashionable, and was becoming a superior suburban
retreat. John Cloake, for example, in <u>The Growth of Richmond</u>
(4) sums up the development of Victorian Richmond in a single
paragraph

The first line from Nine Elms to Richmond was
opened in July 1846 with Richmond Station built
between George Street and Parkshot. The line was
extended to Waterloo and to Staines and Windsor
two years later, and the railway bridge was
constructed close by Asgill House. At once
Richmond embarked on its new career as a dormitory
suburb. New streets were opened up in the old
fields, up the slope of the Hill, off the roads to
London and Mortlake and Kew. New churches were
built to serve the new population centres - St
Matthias on the hill, Christ Church in Kew Road-
and new shopping areas began to develop, for
example in Friars Stile Road and on Sheen
Road.....Within twenty five years of the first
coming of the railway, half the fields of Richmond
had already disappeared under lines of detached or
semi-detached villas, or terraces of smaller
cottages....

Growth and people

The growth of the town during the nineteenth century is best
illustrated through the population and housing statistics
produced by the General Register Office after each census.

Population

	1801	1811	1821	1831	1841	1851
Richmond	4628	5219	5994	7243	7752	9255
Petersham	422	406	516	610	629	653
Kew	424	560	683	837	922	1009

	1861	1871	1881	1891	
Richmond	10926	15113	19066	22684	
Petersham	637	683	566	629	
Kew	1101	1033	1670	2076	(5).

Richmond's population had increased by nearly 20% since 1841,
and by 50% since the first census was taken in 1801. It would
increase by another 18% by 1861. The population of England and
Wales had increased by 12.9% between 1841 and 1851, and by
11.9% between 1851 and 1861 (6). The equivalent population
in 1981 for the two wards of Richmond Hill and Richmond Town,

< 3 >

which approximate the boundary of Richmond between 1801 and 1891, was 14,845 (7).

Growth and houses

Another indicator of the growth of Richmond during the Nineteenth Century is the numbers of houses, built and being built.

Houses inhabited, uninhabited and being built

Richmond	Inhabited	Uninhabited		Being built
1851	1624	44		38
1861	1841	81		31
1871	2566	277		55
1881	3457	238		66
1891	4185	210		33 (5)

There was a 15% increase in the numbers of houses between 1851 and 1861. The General Register Office noted in 1862 that 'The increase in population in Richmond is attributed to the erection of houses since 1851' (8). One of the earliest plots of land to be sold was the land to the east of Queen's Road, which was sold by the Vestry in 1849 in order to pay for a new vicarage for the incumbent of Richmond. Amongst the houses being built at the time of the census was Pembroke Villas on Richmond Green (f95).

Interests and institutions

One can get an idea of the interests of Richmond society in the 1850s from the number of new charities, churches and public institutions established in the decade, reflecting Victorian concern for physical and moral health. According to **Hiscoke's Richmond Almanack** for 1859 (9) the following institutions were founded between 1851 and 1858:

St Matthias Church	consecrated 1858
City Mission School, New Richmond	built 1855
Infant Nursery Servants Home	established 1856
Richmond Young Mans Society	established 1851
Parochial Library and Reading Room	established 1855
Richmond Gas Company	re-established 1853
Richmond Baths and Lavatory Company	established 1855
Richmond Theatre	reopened 1858

The Gas Company was founded in 1847, but was relaunched in 1853 on a grander basis with a new share issue. There was much argument in the town at the time over inadequate water supply, and the construction of new sewers. One sign of this is the number of men whose occupation is listed as 'labourer on the sewers' in the 1851 census, such as John Clifford, William Kilgour and Henry Taylor (f253) or Edward Douglas (f297), who is listed as a 'nightwatchman to sewer builders'.

Health and Wealth

The earliest mortality statistics for the town start in 1874. It is thus difficult to get an idea of how healthy Richmond was in 1851. There was no hospital. The rich could afford to hire nurses. In ED 2C, for example, 16 women are listed as being nurses or nursemaids or 14% of the total number of servants. The number is rather less for the other two

< 4 >

The poor, might get help from one of the charities in the town. The workhouse also acted as a hospital for the incurably ill, the mentally disturbed and the aged.

Lists of people who received indoor relief during 1851 and 1852 are given in the Richmond Union Table of Expenditure (10). According to the Table 181 people were in the workhouse during all or part of 1851/1852. Of this number 32 came from Barnes and Mortlake. The reasons given for their admission to the workhouse were: age 25%; as children 8.8%; illness 27.6%; infirmity and disability 14.7%; unemployment 16%; and other (such as desertion and misconduct) 8.3%.

The Table also indicates that £762 5s 5d was spent on indoor relief for 149 people (1.6% of the population). The Workhouse cost £1860 11s 11d to run during 1851. A further 190 people received outdoor relief, for such reasons as ill health, age, infirmity and to pay for funerals. All in all 3.7% of the total population of Richmond received some form of relief from the Poor Law Overseers. Undoubtedly many people received help from private charities, or through the various almshouses in the town.

S t a t i s t i c a l   s u r v e y

For the purposes of this pamphlet I selected three Enumeration Districts, out of a total of fourteen, containing a cross section of the population of Richmond, to undertake a detailed statistical analysis. The results appear below. Wherever possible I have included a comparison with the figures given in the 1981 Census. The Enumeration Districts (EDs) chosen were 2C, 2E and 2J. The population of all three enumeration districts was 2185 or 23.6% of total population of Richmond. The Districts covered the following areas:

ED 2C (ff79-97) Population 597 (m.250 f.347)

All that part...comprising King Street (SW side), Old Palace Place, Old Friars, Friars Lane, St Helena Terrace, Cholmondely Lodge, Cholmondely Cottage, Queensbury Villa, SW side of the Green, Old Palace Yard, Palace Yard, and the NW side of the Green to the end of Pembroke Terrace, including the Royal Observatory in the Old Park, also the SE side of the Green, called Old Palace Terrace, and round the end of same taking the NW side of Paved Court. (f79)

ED 2E(ff123-149) Population 806 (m.354 f.452)

All that part...comprising the East End of George Street; south side of Square, also the south side of Marshgate from Mr Pullen's garden, Lower George Street (both side) including Union Court, and all yards between the same, south side of George Street, Church Court including Wellington's Yard, the Church Yard wherein is Caroline Place, Church Walk, and Wellington Place, returning down Church Court and Church Walk,

< 5 >

continuing on the south side of George Street, to the
end of High Street (Shore's Joiner) including also
Victoria Place and Artichoke Alley (f123)

ED 2J (ff244-267) Population 782 (m.394 f.388)

All that part...comprising all that plot of houses
called Sheen Dale in the Mortlake Road and also New
Richmond on the South Side of same ending at Coxes
Farm. (f244)

Table 1   Size of Household

Household	(%)ED.2C	ED.2E	ED.2J	Richmond	1981
1	14.2	1.3	18.6	11.4	28.5
2	11.9	11.0	12.6	11.8	34.0
3	11.1	22.1	18.1	17.1	14.9
4	11.9	10.4	16.7	13.0	14.2
5	15.9	11.7	13.1	13.6	5.5
6	7.9	13.0	7.4	9.4	1.7
7	10.3	10.4	5.5	8.7	0.6*
8	7.1	7.8	4.0	6.4	
9	2.5	3.2	4.5	3.4	
10	2.9	2.6	1.0	2.2	
11+	0.5	4.0	5.2	3.2	
TOTAL No	126	154	199		63775
(11)					

* 7 and more people in a household.

Remarkably few people lived alone. Those that did were
often poor and elderly. Large households were made up
of large numbers of children and live-in servants. In
ED2C larger households had a higher ratio of servants
to children. The position was reversed in ED2J. This
is shown in the following table.

Table 2   Households with live-in Servants

ED.2C	ED.2E	ED.2J	Richmond
41.3	26.6	4.5	24.3

Table 3   Age of people

Age (%)	ED.2C	ED.2E	ED.2J	Richmond	1981
0-4	10.0	10.6	16.0	12.2	5.2
5-9	8.6	9.8	14.7	11.0	5.2
10-14	7.5	11.1	12.2	10.3	6.1
15-19	8.4	11.3	7.6	9.1	7.0
20-24	13.1	11.1	5.2	9.8	6.8
25-29	13.0	9.5	7.6	10.0	7.8
30-34	8.6	9.0	6.4	8.0	8.9
35-39	6.5	5.8	6.4	6.2	7.3
40-44	5.4	5.2	6.3	5.6	5.9
45-49	5.4	4.4	4.8	4.9	5.5
50-54	4.3	4.1	5.1	4.5	5.8
55-59	3.5	2.1	2.5	2.7	6.1
60-64	1.9	1.5	1.8	1.7	5.6
65-69	1.2	2.2	1.5	1.6	5.7
70-74	1.4	0.7	0.9	1.0	5.0
75-79	0.5	0.8	0.9	0.7	3.4
80-85	0.5	0.2	0.3	3.3	2.0
85+	0.3	0.0	0.0	0.1	1.2
TOTAL	627	906	787		155161

< 6 >

Table 3 - contd

0-14	26.1	31.5	42.9	33.5	16.5
15-29	34.5	31.9	20.4	28.9	21.6
30-44	20.5	20.0	19.1	19.7	22.1
45-59	13.2	10.6	12.4	12.1	17.4
60-75	4.5	4.4	4.2	4.4	16.3
76+	1.3	1.0	1.2	1.2	6.2

The large number of young people in 1851 is shown in
this table. Generally the people in the wealthy areas
of the town, such as round Richmond Green, lived
longer and had fewer children. In the poorer areas,
such as New Richmond, nearly half the population were
under 15. Very few people lived over 50. (11)

Table 4   Place of Birth

	ED.2C	ED.2E	ED.2J	Richmond
Richmond	26.8	39.0	45.5	37.1
London	18.5	14.6	12.3	15.4
Surrey#	4.5	6.0	4.0	4.8
Middx#	3.1	5.1	3.3	3.8
Parishes adjoining Richmond ##	11.6	7.0	13.8	10.8
Home Counties*	15.8	13.6	11.3	13.6
East Anglia+	1.8	2.1	2.2	2.0
Midlands=	3.6	2.0	2.4	2.7
Northern England**	1.1	1.1	0.5	0.9
West Country++	5.8	6.0	1.8	4.5
Ireland	0.4	1.1	3.0	1.5
Scotland	2.2	0.5	0.1	0.9
Wales	0.9	0.7	0.3	0.6
Europe	1.3	1.3	0.1	0.9
British Colonies	2.4	0.4	0.0	0.9
Other	0.2	0.2	0.2	0.2
TOTAL	551	846	769	(12)

85% of the population came either from Richmond, or
from within 50 miles of the town. Indeed, 47.9% came
either from Richmond or from neighbouring parishes.
Considering the cosmopolitan attractions of the place
it is remarkable how few people originated from
outside the home counties. It is also worth noting
the small percentage of Irish. The great exodus from
Ireland during the Great Famine had not reached the
town. Only one non-European person can definitely be
found in the census returns. She is Sookie (f294),
born in Calcutta.

Table 5   Marital Status (people over 15)

Men

	ED.2C	ED.2E	ED.2J	Richmond	1981
Single	40.6	39.7	32.5	37.6	31.4
Married	54.4	53.7	60.9	56.3	61.3
Widowed	3.8	5.7	6.5	5.2	7.3*
Not Known	1.3	0.9	0.0		
% married/widowed	58.2	59.4	63.3	60.3	68.6
TOTAL	160	229	215		59543

< 7 >

Table 5 - contd
Women

	ED.2C	ED.2E	ED.2J	Richmond	1981
Single	57.5	44.1	18.2	40.0	25.9
Married	32.3	42.7	62.7	45.9	54.1
Widowed	9.8	13.4	17.3	13.5	20.0*
Not Known	0.4	0.0	1.8		
% married/widowed	42.1	56.1	80	59.4	74.1
TOTAL	266	299	220	63821	
% of total pop	71.3	65.5	55.6		79.5

(13) * married or divorced.

The interesting thing to note here is the high proportion of people who never marry. This large number may be due to the proportion of unmarried servants. Women outnumbered men. Taking this into account, it seems more women got married at some time. The high numbers of widows compared to widowers may be because women tended to.live longer. In comparison, however, In Long Buckby, Northants the equivalents were 61% and 67%. In Richmond, Yorks however the figures were 36% and 35.5% (14).

Table 6   Economic activity of adults over 16

Men

	ED.2C	ED.2E	ED.2J	Richmond	1981
Active	93.3	97.4	94.8	95.1	78.4
Inactive	6.7	2.6	5.2	4.8	21.6
TOTAL	163	274	212		

Women

	ED.2C	ED.2E	ED.2J	Richmond	1981
Active	52.6	55.7	43.0	48.6	50.6
Inactive	47.4	44.3	57.0	49.4	49.4
TOTAL	253	280	207		(16)

Unlike many of the large industrial towns there were no areas in Richmond where specific types of work were concentrated. Watermen, however, were often to be found near Water Lane, where the Watermans Arms pub is the only reminder of their presence today. A number of laundresses working at the Royal Laundry lived in the area round Kew Foot Lane, where the Laundry was situated. Workers on the sewers are likely to be found in New Richmond.

Table 8Percentage of women workers over the age of 16 as a total of the adult workforce

	ED.2C	ED.2E	ED.2J	Richmond
	32.0	36.8	30.7	36.6
TOTAL	133	156	89	

This table underestimates the numbers of women working, as a number of girls under 16 were servants. Women were overwhelmingly occupied in three trades as servants, laundresses and washerwomen, and as dressmakers and milliners. In ED 2C some 64% of women workers were servants, and in ED 2E 50%.

< 8 >

Table 7   Employment structure

	ED.2C	ED.2E	ED.2J	Richmond
Professional*	5.1	1.3	0.1	2.2
Clerks=	7.3	7.6	2.3	5.7
Shop owners+	6.2	11.2	2.9	6.7
Shop workers>	3.6	7.6	1.9	4.4
Servants<	41.4	24.8	14.8	27.0
Masters#	3.6	0.4	1.6	1.9
Journeymen@	10.2	2.2	13.2	8.5
Skilled workers&	9.4	16.7	7.1	11.1
Unskilled$	9.1	21.9	51.0	27.3
Child workers[	4.0	6.0	4.2	4.8
TOTAL:	275	447	310	(15)

This table should be treated with some caution. It is not
always possible to determine into which category jobs should
be put. It is also nearly impossible to categorise trades in
order to get a picture of the social structure of Richmond at
this time. In particular it underestimates families of members
of higher social classes who had perhaps only one person
working, but who employed large numbers of servants, as the
table for the size of households shows (Table 2 above).

The majority of the population was employed in satisfying the
needs of the richer elements of society in Richmond, as
servants, working in the building trade, or as shopkeepers and
shop assistants. This is shown by looking at entries in a
trade directory for the town. There are 516 entries William's
Directory for 1850: 44.6% engaged in trade, 23.6% had no
occupation and could be assumed to be of the higher classes,
14.3% were engaged in manufacture, mostly of items for
household use, 7.8% were engaged in service industries, such
as teachers and insurance company representatives, 4.8% as
professionals mostly as doctors or in the law, and 3.9% in
other non-classifiable types of work (17).

T h e   h u m a n   a s p e c t

The Census returns tells us a great deal about individual
residents of Richmond, rich and poor alike. Yet, it takes
reading the Census in conjunction with other documents of the
period to bring the human story alive. Take for example the
two people mentioned in the article by Sir Edward Hertslet
quoted above. The pew opener in 1851 was Mary Stacey (f144),
the collector of the toll on Richmond Bridge was William
Sanders (f162). A couple of the people in the returns have
entries in the Dictionary of National Biography(18), for
example George, Earl of Carlisle, Chancellor of the Duchy of
Lancaster (f57) and his mother Georgina, Dowager Countess of
Carlisle (f8). The poor also have interesting stories to tell.
Take for example Thomas Behanna (f42) a pauper tailor from
Kenway in Cornwall, aged 40, who died destitute in the
Workhouse on 5 April 1851, five days after the Census was
taken (19). Or Amelia Atwood (f167) who during 1851 entered
the Workhouse destitute with a small baby, having been left by
her husband, a whitesmith (10).

Consulting the census returns can leave one wishing to know
more. Why, for example, did James Richardson (f208) combine

< 9 >

the trades of barge builder and bird stuffer. Was Henry
Lascelles (f232) an amusing comic lecturer. Why should Marie
Hylet, age 23 a native of St Malo (f156), should have come to
Richmond to teach French? It might be instructive to talk to
Joseph Bickwell, who at the age of 100 was Richmond's oldest
resident (f38) or some of the older inhabitants about their
memories of England in the late Eighteenth Century.

Some entries in the Returns are misleading. John Currell
(f242) modestly describes himself as a labourer. William's
Directory (17) suggests however that he is an oysterman or
seller. John Abbott (f67) is not a Chinese when he calls
himself a Chinaman. The Directory indicates that he runs a
china and glass warehouse.

Following is a selective list of Richmond's inhabitants in the
Census returns together with the work that they undertook or
some other reason for their inclusion:

folio	name	profession
284	Frederick Ackary	Artist (portrait painter)
240	James Andrews	Collector of Parish Rate
278	Henry Baker	Baronet, Admiral RN, CB
193	Richard Bead	Police Inspector
92	Frederick Benn	Yeast Manufacturer
230	Edmund Bevin	Barrister in actual practise
38	Joseph Bickwell	Pauper: Building Labourer (age 100)
176	Charles Biden	Builder (employing 10 men)
229	Thomas Bisset	Curate of St Johns, Richmond
55	Joseph Bowes	Brewer
261	Thomas Boxhall	Gentleman's servant
215	Frederick Bray	None being a cripple
313	Jane Bray	Builder (employing 15 men)
158	Suzanna Brown	Clear starcher
186	Bryant Budd	Office keeper to the Metropolitan Sewer Commissioners
64	Benjamin Bull	Hotel Keeper, Castle Hotel
243	Martha Bull	Tripe dealer
230	Thomas Bull	Market Gardener (employing 2 men, holding 16 acres)
177	John Burtenshaw	Fly master
136	William Butler	Ostler (conducting tap of Greyhound Hotel)
21	Richard Byam	Rector of Petersham
315	Augusta Cambridge	Duchess of Cambridge
282	John Chant	Relieving Officer
17	John Cheesman	Gas Fitter
201	Elizabeth C. Child	Marriage settlement
306	Joseph Childs	Smith and bellhanger
186	Alfred Christopher	Curate, St Johns
135	Thomas Clark	Chymist (sic) and Dentist
183	Katherine Clifton	Schoolmistress, Royal Naval School
197	Thomas Cockerill	Superintendent of the Royal Laundry
326	Charles Cole	Clerk in Public Record Office
104	Charlotte Collins	Interest of money
104	Edward Collins	Brewery and maltster (employing 27 men)

< 10 >

240	Thomas Cooper	Superintendant of Railway Station
279	Robert Cope	Porter at Hickey's Almshouses, late a baker
141	James Costelow	Omnibus proprietor
236	John Covington	Occasional servant
328	William Crampten	Dentist
306	Joseph Crandley	Coach trimmer
316	John Smith	Curator of Kew Gardens
161	Evan Davies	Independent Minister
302	Walter Demergue	Curate of Richmond
297	Edward Douglas	Night watchman to sewer builders
86	Edwin Downs	Brewer and Lighterman
87	Henry Downs	Lighterman and Maltster (employing 52 men)
88	William Doyle	Of unsound mind
83	John Dundas	Baronet, Captain RN on halfpay
315	Mary Edge	Shareholder in gas business
241	William Edwards	Builder (Master employing 30 men)
235	William Eldridge	Letter carrier, HM Service
6	Joseph Ellis	Hotel Keeper: Star and Garter Hotel
133	Ann Everett	Dairy Woman
34	Georgina Exmouth	Viscountess of Exmouth
158	Trehusion(?) Faenza	Roman Catholic priest
338	Ebenezer Ferme	JP
177	Richard Filkin	Surgeon, MRCS Edin. Army surgeon on halfpay
168	David Findhope	Veterinary Surgeon
58	John Finlaison	Actuary of the National Debt
285	Lettice Flower	Fancy basket maker
187	Albany Foublanque	Clerk to Board of Trade
304	George Foy	Assistant in fancy warehouse
106	Elizabeth Franklin	Schoolmistress (age 78)
178	Elizabeth Friend	Gentlewoman, fundholder
189	Charles Fuller	Grazier
107	Samuel Gaines	Gaslighter
52	Francis Gainfield	Artist
333	William Gale	Plumber (employing 5 men)
233	William Grarhalgh	Zinc worker (Journeyman)
32	Peter Bramer Hall	Manufacturer of gunpowder
175	James Harrington	Tobacco pipe manufacturer (employing 4 men and 2 boys)
238	Charles Harrison	Electric engineer
239	Joseph Harrison	Writer, horticulture and floriculture, nurseryman
155	William Harvey	Artist, painter and designer
333	Mary Hawes	Gatekeeper, Royal Pleasure Grounds
159	Isaac Head	Hackney Coach driver
92	Sarah Head	Straw Bonnet Manufacturer
296	Elizabeth Hendery	Has been a servant (age 23)
38	Thomas Heydrick	Master Richmond Workhouse
327	John Higgins	Parish beadle
158	Robert Hodgson	Roman Catholic priest
299	John Hope	Architect and surveyor
8	Mary Howard	Lady Mary Howard
295	John Hyde	JP for Manchester. Proprietor of land, houses and coal mines
2	Louise Islip	Teacher of the French Language
74	George Jackson	Lighterman (employing 1 man and 1

< 11 >

		apprentice)
37	Samuel Jackson	Governor of Weslyan College
83	William Jacobs	Billiard Marker, Old Ship Hotel
249	Edward Jeffries	Stoker at gasworks
68	Edward Jefs	JP, Surveyor of Her Majesty's Lands
211	Thomas Johnson	Sheep master (employing 1 man and 1 boy)
212	James Keen	Grocer and tea dealer (employing 2 men)
92	Cornelius Kemp	Musician and Waterman
43	Edward Kerriston	Baronet, MP, Lieutenant General
182	Henry Charles Lacy	JP. MP for Lancaster
57	Caroline Lamb	Widow, Hon George Lamb
254	Reuben Langford	Railway engine cleaner
237	Charles Langston	Parish beadle
282	Samuel Le Blond	Independent Minister, East Sheen Chapel
335	Edith Lewes	Nursechild (Age 5 months)
238	William Little	Herbalist
140	Edmund Lloyd	Chymist (sic) and Post Master
164	William Long	Builder (employing 7 men)
6	John Lucas	Park Keeper to Her Majesty
191	Emery (?) Lucis	Laundress to the Queen
280	Arthur Lysaght	Rear Admiral RN
198	James Mackay	Teaching classics and mathematics
253	William Mackay	Foreman at Kew Gardens
94	Richard Macklin	Photographic artist at Royal Observatory
131	Amy Marchant	Confectioner
254	John Marchant	Hawker of vegetables
201	Elizabeth Marriott	Cook at Royal Laundry
275	William Martin	Author, educational and scientific
134	Charles Mayne	Fruiterer and Greengrocer (employing 18 men and 4 boys)
16	Sarah Middleship	In charge of Her Majesty's Cottage, Kew Gardens
219	Thomas Moseley	Pensioner East India Company Service
141	Elizabeth Neville	Assistant to father (a butcher)
169	Frederick Newby	Egg and butter hawker
130	Mary Palmer	Relief from parish (age 74)
230	Thomas Parkin	Retired sadler
155	Mary Peacock	Companion
207	Joseph Peirce	Ironmonger and smith (employing 14 men)
112	William Peters	Corndealer
138	Mary Pigott	Tuition at home (age 11)
171	John Pollard	Tailor and habit maker
300	Thomas Pressley	Light porter. Has been a livery servant
17	Edward Price	Chaplain to Richmond Union Workhouse
197	Morgan Price	Cattle Doctor
177	Thomas Price	JP. Landed proprietor
332	Margaret Print	Dressmaker (employing 3 women)
316	Mary Murphy	Queen's housekeeper (Age 80)
10	Caroline Queensbury	Marchioness of Queensbury
168	George Ramsay	Coachmaker (employing 6 men)
214	Phebe Reading	Garden woman
133	Alice Reeds	Apprentice to Dairy Trade

< 12 >

230	Sir Thomas Reeve	JP
142	Lucy Richardson	Mangling
324	Joseph Rigby	Contractor for public (?) employing 2180 men
317	Henry Rigge	Perfurmer employing 4 men
300	Robert Roberts	Cigar manufacturer
274	James Robinson	Builder and Tile Kilner at Brentford (employing 40 men)
171	Christopher Rokins	Hawker of fish
228	Ambrose Rowles	Chimney sweeper
101	Robert Rowse	Not in Business: refuses to state source of income
220	William Scott	Sergeant and Regimental Clerk, Army
317	Charles Servis	Artist
197	Ann Shaftesbury	Countess of Shaftesbury
45	Elizabeth Shaw	Dealer in Pastry
116	Henry Sheen	Painter and musician
165	Eliza Shott	Ironer
172	Benjamin Silvester	Horsekeeper
128	Mary Simmons	Plumber (employing 2 men)
174	William Slade	Marine Store Dealer
296	'Captain' Smith	Not known
282	Frederick Smith	Assistant Curate of Richmond
119	George Smith	Lamplighter
129	Henry Smith	Police Officer
314	Charlotte Sowter	Fruiterer and lodging housekeeper
61	John Spalding	Fishing Tackle Manufacturer
197	Thomas Spury	Gentleman. Income from property on Court of Chancery
148	Thomas Stacey	Tobacco pipe manufacturer
188	Susan Stanford	Cowkeeper (employing 4 men, 1 woman, farming 16 acres)
116	Joseph Staples	Ladies shoemaker (employing 6 men)
232	Thomas Stapleton	Coachman HM Service
273	Benjamin Staveley	File cutter and Chelsea Pensioner
230	George Steele	Nurseryman (employing 4 men)
36	James Stephen	Professor of Modern History, Cambridge, PC, KCB
252	Charles Stevens	Labourer on roads (age 77)
60	Elizabeth Stevens	Corset and Umbrella Maker
250	'Infant'Thatcher	(age under 1 month)
194	James Thompson	Chelsea Pensioner, Sergeant 1st Surrey Militia
106	James Thompson	Journeyman Houseprints
161	Edmund Tipping	City missionary
233	William Towers	Relief from Parish. Formerly worked on roads
231	Arthur Turner	French polisher (Master)
13	Hester Veale	Pew Opener
298	Ann Waters	Sailor's wife
235	John Welch	Practising Special Pleader
86	Nancy Wells	Pensioner RN
94	John Welsh	Scientific Observer at Royal Observatory

< 13 >

162	Thomas Wheatley	Sexton
335	Mary Ann White	Servant out of work (age 16)
196	Richard Willis	Manufacturing jeweller (employing 60 men and women)
9	William Winch	Barge Horse Master (employing 3 men)
285	William Woodruff	Chairmaker and Turner
118	Ann Louise Yeates	No occupation (age 30 daughter)

N o t e s

(1) Robert Lundie's Railway Excurtionist's Handbook to Richmond, Kew and Hampton Court (London, 1851) p10

(2) A Guide to Kew, Richmond, Twickenham and Hampton Court (London, 1859) p22-23

(3) Richmond History Collection Cuttings Vol 4, p57-58.

(4) The Growth of Richmond (Paper No 1, Richmond Society Historical Section, 1982) p30

(5) Registration and Poor Law Districts: Censuses of 1861-1891. Figures for 1801-1851 to be found in a note in HO 107/1605 f1.

(6) figures given in The Rise of Suburbia ed. F.M.L. Thompson (Leicester, 1982) p34.

(7) 1981 figures from 1981 Census: Key Facts and Figures (LB Richmond, 1982), p3

(8) Registration and Poor Law Districts: Census of England and Wales 1861 p236.

(9) Hiscoke's Richmond Almanack, 1859

(10) Richmond Union Table of Expenditure, 1852

(11) 1981 figures from Census 1981: County Report: Greater London (HMSO, 1982) Table 7, p42

(12)
\#   excluding parts in London
\#\#   Barnes, Brentford, Chiswick, Ham, Hammersmith, Hampton, Isleworth, Kew, Kingston, Mortlake, Petersham, Putney, Sheen, Teddington, Twickenham
*   Berkshire, Buckinghamshire, Essex, Hampshire, Hertfordshire, Kent, Oxfordshire, Sussex
\+   Bedfordshire, Cambridgeshire, Huntingdonshire, Norfolk, Suffolk
\-   Derbyshire, Herefordshire, Leicestershire, Lincolnshire, Northamptonshire, Nottinghamshire, Rutland, Shropshire, Staffordshire, Warwickshire, Worcestershire
**   Cheshire, Cumberland, Durham, Lancashire, Northumberland, Westmorland, Yorkshire
\+\+   Cornwall, Devon, Dorset, Gloucestershire, Wiltshire

(13) 1981 figures from Census 1981: County Report: Greater London (HMSO, 1982) Table 7, p42

< 14 >

Notes - contd

(14) Quoted in <u>A Guide to the Nineteenth Century Census Enumerators' Books</u> (Open University, 1982) p15

(15)

* Landowners, Officers, merchants, employers of 10 men or more

\- Clerks, teachers, employers of 9 men and less

\+ Shop owners, landlords, keepers of lodging houses

\> shop men, bar and hotel workers, milliners

< Butlers, cooks, footmen, gardeners, general servants, house keepers,housemaids, house servants, nursemaids, nurses, other servants

Masters painters, butchers, etc

@ Journeymen in building trades, the service industries etc

& Dressmakers, boot makers, smiths and other people with some skill in the trade

$ Labourers, agricultural labourers and other unskilled workers

[Errand boys, apprentices, and other young workers. But not including young servants.

(16) <u>Active</u> is defined as people over the age of 16 engaged in work. <u>Inactive</u> is defined as people who are unemployed, receive a pension or some form of unearned income, or are retired.

(17) <u>William's Directory for 1850</u>

(18) <u>Dictionary of National Biography</u> (Vol X, p19)

(19) <u>Richmond Union Admission and Discharge Book</u> for 1851

Sources numbers 1, 2, 3, 4, 7, 9, 10, 13, 17, 18, 19 can be consulted either in the Local History Room or the Reference Library at the Old Town Hall, Whittaker Avenue, Richmond.

Acknowledgements: Thanks to the overworked and understaffed librarians in the Local History Library for their assistance. Quotations from the Census Returns are Crown Copyright.

Street and Surname Indexes

How to use the indexes

1) Street index

All the streets in Richmond, Petersham and Kew, together with public houses, schools, other public institutions, and detached houses listed by the enumerator are indexed in alphabetical order together with the folio numbers where they may be found in the returns. Thus if one wanted to look at

< 15 >

George Yard, Richmond the index shows that entries are to be found on folio 130. Public houses are abbreviated as PH.

2) Surname index

This is a list of people in surname order, together with the folio or folios where they are to be found. Only surnames are given. No other details, such as first names or age, are included. Like surnames may well appear more than once on a folio, but will be only listed once.

Surnames are listed here as they appear in the original census returns. The hand writing of some of the enumerators is difficult to read. If a name is unclear it is marked with a (?) in the index. The enumerator may also have misspelt names, so it is important to look at all variants.

P i e c e   a n d   f o l i o   n u m b e r s

If you wish to refer to a return in a book please quote the piece and folio numbers. This means that other people will be able to find the return easily. The PRO piece number for these returns is HO 107/1605.

Folio numbers are stamped numbers on the top right hand corner of alternative pages of the census returns. They cover two sides of paper. If there is a reference to folio 328 look both at page stamped 328, and the page following.

A r e a   c o v e r e d

In the returns, the Parish of Petersham is to be found on folios 1-22, Richmond on folios 23-309, and Kew on folios 310-338. The areas covered are based on the traditional Parish boundaries.

A c c u r a c y

This index is as accurate as possible. It is inevitable however that a few errors have crept in. Please note there is no page 22 in the Surname Index. This is due to an error. No entries however are missing from the index as a result.

If you spot a mistake please contact Simon Fowler, 13 Grovewood, Sandycombe Rd, Kew, Richmond, Surrey, TW9 3NF

[Biographical note: Simon Fowler has worked at the Public Record Office since 1979. At present he is the Officer in Charge of the Census Room at Portugal Street.]

< 16 >

Street	HO 107/1605	folios
Castle Hotel	64-65	
Castle PH	259	
Castle Stables	68	
Castle Terrace	68-69	
Castle Yard, Hill Street	68	
Cedar Grove	93	
Chapel House, Vineyard	158	
Chapel Yard, Kew Foot Lane	190-191	
Childs Alley, Kew Road	228-229	
Cholmondely Cottage	87	
Cholmondely Lodge	87	
Church Almshouses, Marshgate Road	279	
Church Cottage	164	
Church Court	146-147	
Church House, Red Lion Street	164	
Church Row	174-175	
Church Walk	143-144	
Clarence House School, Vineyard	157	
Clarence Street	200-202, 213-214	
Clarence Terrace	63-64	
Compasses PH	48	
Craven Cottage, Kew Foot Lane	196	
Crawford Cottage	36	
Cricketeers Tavern, Richmond Green	105-106	
Crofton Arms PH	247-248	
Crofton Terrace	248-256	
Cumberland Buildings	333-338	
Cumberland Cottage, Richmond Road	333	
Cumberland Place, Richmond Road	331-332	
Days Cottages	262	
Devonshire Cottage, Lower Road	57	
Devonshire House, Gardeners Cottage	8	
Doughty House, The Terrace	35-36	
Downe House, The Terrace	34-36	
Downes Buildings	172-173	
Duke Street	115, 207	
Dunstable House, Marshgate Road	278	
Dunstable Lodge School, Marshgate Road	276-277	
Dunstable Place, Marshgate Road	278-279	
Dysart Arms PH	9	
Economical Coffee House, Kew Road	243	
Eglantine Cottages	323	
Eliza Cottage, St John's Grove	199	
Ellerker House, The Hill	32	
Elm Cottage, Ham Road	19-20	
Everalls Cottages	263	
Farm House	13	
Flora Cottage, Kew Road	239	
Folley Cottage, Duke Street	207	
Foresters Arms PH, Kew Road	241	
Fox and Duck PH	14	

Street	HO 107/1605	folios
Friars Lane	86-87	
Friars Style Road	33	
Frogmore Cottage, Mortlake Lane	238	
Garden Cottage, Ormond Row	176	
Gate Lodge, Richmond Park	6	
Genua Villa, Marshgate Road	280	
George Street	109-116, 119, 121, 132, 134-141	
George Yard	130	
Gloster Cottages, Richmond Road	329	
Gloster House School, Richmond Road	329-330	
Gloster Row, Richmond Road	330-331	
Gloucester House, The Hill	33	
Gloucester Villas	33	
Golden Square	120	
Goslings Court	121	
Gothic Cottage, Kew Foot Lane	192	
Green	182	
Greenside	121-122	
Grove Cottage, Kew Foot Lane	193	
Grove Lodge	281	
Grove Terrace, Night and Morning Row	217	
Halford Place	162-163	
Halls Cottages, Clarence Street	202	
Ham House	21	
Ham Road	19-23	
Hanover Cottage	315	
Hanover House	316	
Hanover Lodge	316-317	
Hanover Place, Richmond Road	328-329	
Harbord House, The Hill	44	
Haverfield House, Kew Green	325	
Hermitage, Church Row	175	
Heron House, Hill Street	63	
Hickey's Almshouses, Marshgate Road	279-280	
High Rd	14	
Hill Lodge, Upper Hill Street	47	
Hill Place	53	
Hill Rise	44-45	
Hill Road	30-31	
Hill Street	63-68	
Hill, The	36, 43-44	
Holbrook House	28	
Holme Cottage	294-295	
Hope PH, Kew Road	227	
Hotham House	63	
Houblon's Almshouses	308-309	
Husey's Cottage, Kew Foot Lane	192	
Jessamine Cottages, Friars Style Road	33	
John's Cottages, Richmond Road	333	
Joy Cottage, Kew Foot Lane	196	
Joys Alley, Kew Foot Lane	191-192	

Street	HO 107/1605	folios
Keepers House, Richmond Park		6
Kew Foot Lane		189-197, 202-203
Kew Gardens		316
Kew Green		313-327, 338
Kew Lodge, Kew Road		230
Kew Observatory, Old Deer Park		94
Kew Palace		316
Kew Palace Lodge		316
Kew Priory		327
Kew Road		207-212, 226-231, 235-243
Kew Wharf Road		319-320
King Street		82-85, 108-109
Kings Head PH, By the Bridge		61
Kings Head PH, George Street		109
Laburnham Cottage, Paradise Road		161
Lancaster Cottages		160-161
Lancaster Place		31-32
Lansdowne House, The Hill		44
Lansdowne Place, Lower Road		56
Larkfield Lodge, Kew Road		238-239
Lass of Richmond Hill PH		43
Laurel Cottage, St John's Grove		197-198
Lemon Tree PH, Kew Road		241
Lewis Place, Kew Road		212-213
Lichfield House, Marshgate Road		275
Lion Cottage, Kew Road		236
Lion Lodge, Kew Road		235-236
Lion Row		274
Little George Street		132-134
Little Green		182-185
Longs Cottages		263-264
Lower Road		47-48, 52-59
Lumley Lodge		239
Magpie PH		118
Maids of Honour Row		88-89
Manor House, Marshgate Road		280-281
Manor House, River Lane		12
Manor House Stables, Marshgate Road		281
Mansfield House, The Hill		36
Marlborough Cottages		296-299
Marshgate		126-129, 301-302
Marshgate House School, Marshgate Road		275-276
Marshgate Road		273-285
Martins Buildings		262-263
Michael Place		21
Michel Place		156-157
Michels Almshouses		157
Mitchells Terrace, Kew Foot Lane		194
Montrose House		11
Mortlake Lane		238, 327
Mortlake Road		261-262
Mount Ararat		153

Street	HO 107/1605	folios
Mount Ararat Lane	153	
Mount Ararat Lodge School	154	
Mount Pleasant, Marshgate Road	283-284	
Myrtle Cottage, Kew Foot Lane	196	
New Grove House, Kew Foot Lane	192	
New Ship PH, King Street	84	
Night and Morning Row	216-221	
Nightingale Cottage, The Hill	44	
North West of Square	207	
Old Court House, The Green	94	
Old Deer Park	189	
Old Friars	85-86	
Old Palace Lane	90	
Old Palace Terrace	94-96	
Old Palace Yard	89-90	
Old Palace, Palace Green	85	
Old Ship PH	82	
Old Worple Way	302-307	
Oliver Cottage, Kew Foot Lane	193	
Orange Tree PH, Kew Road	209	
Ormond Cottage, Ormond Road	175	
Ormond Lodge, Ormond Row	176	
Ormond Row	175-178	
Pagoda Cottage, Kew Road	230	
Pagoda House, Kew Road	230	
Pagoda Lodge, Kew Road	237	
Paradise Cottage, Paradise Road	161	
Paradise Place	163	
Paradise Road	161-162	
Paradise Terrace	161-162	
Paragon	57-58	
Park Cottage	328	
Park Place	21	
Park Place, Kew Foot Lane	193	
Park Road Mews	296	
Park Villas	293-294	
Parkshot	186-189	
Park Villa, Kew Foot Lane	192	
Paved Court	96-97, 107-108	
Peldon	281-282	
Pembroke Cottage, Richmond Park	6	
Pembroke Lodge, Richmond Park	6	
Pembroke Terrace	93	
Pensioners Court	119-120	
Percy Yard, Lower Road	54	
Petersham Lodge, River Lane	12	
Police Station, Princes Street	289	
Pooles Houses, Back Rd	18	
Porters Gate, Pembroke Lodge, Richmond Park	6	
Post Office, Petersham	17	
Princes Head PH, Richmond Green	107	

Street	HO 107/1605	folios
Princes Street		287-288
Priory Lodge, Kew Green		324-325
Prospect House, Upper Hill Street		28
Prospect Lodge, Vineyard		155
Prospect Place		170A-172
Queen Elizabeth Almshouses		155-156
Queen's Dairy, Parkshot		188
Queen's School, Kew Green		324
Queens Road		36-43
Queensbury Cottage		86
Queensbury Place		86
Queensbury Villa		87
Railway Hotel, Kew Road		239
Railway Tavern, Kew Road		239
Railway Tavern, New Richmond		256
Red Cow PH, Marshgate Road		284
Red Lion Lane		174
Red Lion PH, Red Lion Street		170A
Red Lion Street		164-170A
Reeve's Cottages		248
Resolution Court		120-121
Retreat Cottage, Paradise Road		161
Richmond Green		101-107
Richmond Hill, Petersham		8
Richmond House, Upper Hill Street		28
Richmond Road, Kew		313, 327-333
Richmond Road Alms Houses, Petersham		8
River Lane		11-12
River Side		323
Riverdale House, Lower Road		57
Royal Laundry, Kew Foot Lane		197
Robinson Brick Fields		300
Roebuck Tap PH, The Terrace		34
Roebuck Tavern PH, The Terrace		34-35
Rose Cottage, Petersham		9
Rose Cottage, Friars Style Road		33
Rose Cottage Hotel, Friars Style Road		33
Rose Cottage, Kew Foot Lane		194
Rose Cottage, Kew Road		226, 230
Rose Cottage, River Lane		12
Rosedale School, Kew Foot Lane		195-196
Rothsay Villas		298-299
Royal Hotel		63
Royal Hotel Tap		62
Royal Naval School, Little Green		183-185
Royal Oak, Bottens Place		259
Royal Terrace		61-62
Rutland Lodge		11
St George Place		173-174
St Helena Terrace		86-87
St John's Brewery, Kew Road		212

Street	HO 107/1605	folios
St John's Passage, Kew Road		229
St John's Place		231-239
St John's Grove		197-200
Sandpits		17-19
Sandpitts Cottage		17
Sandy Lane		238, 281
School House, Church Row		174-175
School House, West Sheen Vale		261
School, 10-11 Parkshot		187
School, Clarence Street		213
School, Lower Road		52-54
Sheen Dale		247
Sheen Vale		76-78
Sheen Villas		295
Spread Eagle Inn		65
Spring Farm		307-308
Spring Grove		281
Spring Terrace		300-301
Square, North West of		207
See also The Square		
Square, South Side		131-132
Stable Yard, Nightingale Lane		44
Stafford Mews		42
Stafford Place		43
Stanley Cottage		36
Star and Garter Hotel		6-8
Steeles Gardens (?), Kew Foot Lane		197
Sudbrooke Cottage, Sudbrooke Lane		14
Sudbrooke House, Sudbrooke Park		5
Sudbrooke Lane		14-16
Sudbrooke Park Lodge		5
Suffield House, Paradise Road		161
Sun Inn, Parkshot		189
Sweeps Alley, Back of Bank		215-216
Syon House, The Hill		36
Talbot Stables		69
Talbot Tap PH		69
Tam O'Shanter PH, Kew Road		211
Terrace House		34
The Green		88, 96
The Palace, Palace Green		85
The Recess, The Hill		36
The Rise		26-28
The Square		272-273
Theatre		93
Three Pigeons PH, Lower Road		56
Tudor Cottage		295
Tudor House		88
Tudor Lodge		88
Twenty Row		264-267
Union Court		129-130
Upper Hill Street		26, 28-31, 44-47, 59-60

Verandah Cottage, Hill Road	30	
Verandah House, The Green	96	
Verulam Cottage, Upper Hill Street	31	
Victoria Cottage, Kew Foot Lane	193	
Victoria Place	147	
Villa Retreat, Friars Lane	· 86	
Vine Cottage	155	
Vine Cottages	295	
Vine Row	158-160	
Vineyard	154-158	
Vineyard House School, Vineyard	155, 298-299	
Vineyard Lodge School	163-164	
Violet Cottage, Kew Road	240	
Water Lane	69-73	
Waterloo Place	285-287	
Waterloo Place, Kew	321-322	
Wellington Place	141-143	
Wellington Yard	141	
Wentworth House	94	
Wesleyan Theological Institution, Queens Road	37-38	
Weslyan College Lodge	38	
West Sheen Vale	259-261	
Wheatsheaf PH, Kew Road	229-230	
White Cross Buildings	74-75	
White Cross Row	74, 76	
White Cross, Waterside	74	
White Hart Inn	66	
Wilds Cottage	300	
Wilsons Buildings	225-226	
Woods House, Clarence Street	202	
Woodbine Cottage, Ham Road	20	
Workhouse	38-42	
York Cottages	31	
York House, Hill Road	30	
York Place, Hill Road	30-31	
York Villas, Hill Road	30	

Surname	folios
Abarve	185
Abbott	26, 67, 110, 131, 139, 194
Ackary	283, 284
Ackerman	284
Ackland	74
Adams	32, 93, 137, 195, 227, 308, 327
Addis	317
Addison	197
Afford	41
Agate	138
Aisten	202
Aiters	71
Aiton	43
Akerman	60
Akers	302
Albertuzzi	127
Albrighton	37
Alder	82, 256
Alderson	307
Alderton	314, 328
Aldridge	161, 316, 331
Alexander	113, 329, 330
Allam	146
Allen	27, 95, 157, 175, 239, 277, 301, 316, 334
Allistone	219
Alloway	19
Allum	9
Alston	33
Alum	148
Amador	53
Amato	127
Amos	32
Amswick	186
Anderson	31, 57, 64, 113, 153, 214
Andionde	329
Andrewes	7
Andrews	7, 29, 44, 55, 88, 102, 127, 135, 168, 189, 240, 280, 321
Angless	257, 272, 273
Annandale	40
Ansell	11, 294
Anthony	302, 303
Antil	274
Aoliar (?)	8
Apps	193
Arbridge	27
Archbold	314
Archer	143
Aris	112, 115, 142, 143, 309
Arkwell	295
Armitage	317
Armstrong	43
Arnold	6, 12, 96, 189

Surname	folios
Arnon	88
Arnott	26, 132
Arthur	63
Artlebury	8, 13
Ascedeshine	64
Asgue	299
Ash	115
Ashbee	13
Ashbourner	5
Ashburne	315, 331
Ashburnham	44
Ashby	15, 142
Ashop	53
Ashworth	163
Askey	7, 68
Asley	301
Assen	187
Aston	274
Atkins	93
Atkinson	5, 318
Attearly	319
Attewell	176
Attfield	35, 113, 279
Attkins	232
Atwood	167
Austen	7, 107
Austin	273, 285, 295
Avery	32, 159
Avins	300
Ayars	64, 65, 68
Ayers	41, 64, 89
Ayles	13
Aylin	185
Aylwyn	132
Ayres	27, 157
Babington	301
Bacon	38, 96, 140
Bagley	32, 304, 305
Bagnoll	117, 119, 199
Bagwell	236, 327
Baidrick	324
Bail	274
Bailey	6, 19, 41, 43, 102, 118, 147, 175, 182, 183
Baillie	122, 298
Baily	56, 307
Bainbridge	53
Baines	215, 314
Bainsfather	201
Baitham	69
Baker	7, 20, 56, 73, 103, 135, 138, 163, 170, 177, 212, 230, 233, 234, 248, 257, 261, 276, 278, 294, 317, 332

Surname	folios
Bakewell	338
Balchin	173
Baldock	31, 164, 277, 305
Baldry	160
Baldwin	58, 134, 211, 259, 304, 327
Bales	275, 278
Ball	88, 214, 236, 250, 275
Ballard	121, 169, 302
Baly	281
Bamford	138, 164
Banes	6
Barber	28, 52, 94, 126, 226, 238, 239
Barclay	183
Barett	280
Barfoot	190
Barke	89
Barker	85, 131, 284
Barling	144
Barlow	282
Barly	280
Barnard	131, 178
Barnes	65, 87, 116, 215, 219
Barnett	254, 255, 298, 317
Barney	210
Barnford	109
Barnstock	280
Barolins	113
Barratt	187
Barraty	17
Barrett	136, 143, 331
Barrey	184
Barrilli	128
Barry	53, 162, 239
Bartes	120
Bartlett	94
Barton	189, 202, 277, 289
Bartram	176, 272
Barvell	103
Bass	175, 320, 324
Bassett	37, 256, 282
Batchelor	8, 241
Bateman	31, 95
Bates	66, 156
Bath	195
Bathews	235
Bathurst	89
Batten	86, 202
Batty	39
Baulay	88
Baxter	330, 331
Bayley	105, 255
Bayly	275
Baynton	184
Beach	10, 305, 306

Surname	folios
Beacham	61
Beacon (?)	76
Beaman	58
Beard	107, 193, 252
Beare	145, 217
Beatt	56
Beauchamp	139
Beaujeau	127
Beaumont	93, 295
Beaver	293
Beavis	43, 44
Beazelly	68
Beazley	258
Beben	178
Beck	301
Becke	275
Beckenham	172
Beckett	6
Beckingham	319
Bedding	44
Beddingfield	317
Bedward	127, 194, 195, 272
Bedwell	164
Bee	12
Beecher	278
Beeney	115
Beever	294
Begby	297
Begent	116, 117
Behanna	42
Bell	10, 44, 73, 89, 111, 162, 194, 277, 308, 331
Bellamy	67
Beller	87
Bendy	88
Benfield	164
Bengant	37
Benn	92
Bennett	36, 304
Benneworth	141
Benskins	58
Benson	195
Bentley	58
Berridge	242
Berry	44, 187, 240
Berthon	60
Berwick	316
Beseley	336
Besley	28
Best	29, 278
Bettis	175
Bevin	230
Bewhardt	53
Bickwell	38
Bidault	127

Surname	folios
Biden	176
Bienery	280
Bigard	105
Biggs	45, 76
Bignell	160
Billett	65
Binfield	38
Binns (?)	327
Birch	11, 59, 95, 105, 170, 177
Bird	17, 21, 43, 154, 157, 170, 170a, 299
Birgasse	53
Bishop	154, 233, 260, 325
Bisset	229
Bisshopp	89
Bizlear (?)	118
Black	167
Blackall	263
Blackbourn	211
Blackburne	137
Blackett	87
Blackford	15
Blackman	66, 174, 216
Blackshaw	10
Blake	74, 187, 321
Blanch	61
Blanchard	242
Blarland	68
Blazeley	135
Blegg	336
Blincowe	256
Blizard	32, 35, 186
Bloom	69
Blowfield	8
Blujeau	54
Blundell	39, 41, 313, 338
Blunt	107, 160
Blyth	95, 157
Boarn	330
Bobinson	293
Boddy	199, 235, 242, 247, 304
Boldocini	53
Bolton	40, 213, 331
Bond	87, 139, 144, 211, 265, 266, 302, 317, 335, 337
Bonell	153
Bonner	155
Bookwright	36
Boon	215
Borley	144, 170
Borradaile	298
Bosher	58, 305
Boston	129, 288
Boswell	330
Bosworth	10
Bott	29

Surname	folios
Botten	247
Boules	230
Bourke	289
Bourne	53
Boutflower (?)	103
Bowden	264
Bower	53
Bowler	212
Bowles	55, 85, 92
Bowley	83
Bowman	48, 195
Bown	158
Bowner	46
Bowry	228
Boxall	321
Boxer	183
Boxhall	261
Boxshall	258
Boyd	9, 324
Boyle	127
Bracher	64
Brackley	243
Bradford	64
Bradley	127, 294
Bradshaw	8, 35, 116, 209
Braff	131
Bragg	214, 215
Brambleby	111
Branchley	174
Brand	315
Branesgrove	96
Branson	154, 159
Branston	36
Brasell	337
Brass	207
Braud	184, 185
Bray	313
Brazier	46, 184, 247
Breadmore	60, 170a
Brecall (?)	104
Bremer	155
Brenchley	6, 136
Brennan	232
Brewer	33, 60, 67, 109, 117, 161
Brewhouse	55
Brice	106
Brichett	112
Bricket	77
Brickford	86
Bricknell	162, 188
Brickwell	60, 329
Bridges	44, 89
Brigg	89
Briggs	172, 249

Surname	folios
Bright	215
Brine	301
Briscoe	164, 189
Brise	72
Bristow	38, 135, 185, 229
Brittain	46, 47
Britton	140
Broad	110, 209
Broadstead	86
Broadway	135
Brocket	97
Brockey	95, 170a
Brockill	42
Brockley	144
Broderick	278
Bronnen	231
Brooker	32
Brookes	109, 258
Brooks	41
Broom	35, 233
Broomfield	149
Broughton	82, 140
Brown	14, 17, 20, 29, 33, 36, 44, 60, 89, 108, 109, 128, 141, 146, 175, 176, 196, 199, 209, 212, 216, 238, 277, 279, 286, 299, 309
Brownage	45
Browne	284, 321
Browning	95, 119, 185, 329
Brownrigg	321
Bruce	53, 102
Brusted (?)	199
Bryan	68
Bryant	59
Buchanan	183
Buck	53, 138, 301
Buckby	195
Buckland	255
Buckle	12, 168
Buckner	288
Budd	104, 148, 169, 183, 186, 273, 296
Bugby	139
Bull	58, 64, 104, 175, 230, 240, 243, 263, 276, 284
Bullen	320
Buller	233
Bullin	231
Bullock	39
Bulpin	134
Bulworthy	34
Bunce	77
Bunker	66
Bunn	69, 76, 212
Buntin	238
Bunting	243
Burbridge	28, 297, 334

Surname	folios
Churchouse	127
Chuter	278
Clack	317
Clapperton	183
Clapshaw	163
Clark	146, 191, 210, 213, 287, 319, 325
Clarke	10, 53, 127, 135, 138, 166, 176, 200, 288
Clay	236, 240
Claydon	28, 276
Clayton	323
Cleasby	189
Cleaver	328
Clement	12
Clewley	331
Cliff	119
Clifford	250, 253
Clifton	14, 18, 183
Clinch	209
Cluer	169
Coaleman (?)	167
Cock	187
Cockayne	318
Cockerill	197
Cocks	184
Coghlan	199
Cohen	330
Colborn	278
Colbourne	297
Cole	20, 30, 136, 299, 323, 336
Coleman	214, 287
Colines	166
Collard	300
Collerell	324
Collett	186, 232
Collier	198, 199
Collings	193
Collins	16, 33, 62, 104, 139, 185, 212, 308, 337
Collis	117
Colman	27, 35, 54
Colquhan	277
Colston	193
Colyer	127, 305
Comfort	293
Connell	299
Connor	264
Conroy	102, 106
Conybeare	325
Cook	120, 135, 166, 168, 235, 279, 301, 307, 318, 332
Cooke	10, 63, 102, 308
Coole	236
Coombes	117
Coombs	200, 220
Cooper	28, 32, 35, 37, 39, 40, 46, 55, 63, 67, 107, 113, 122, 138, 158, 170, 170a, 200, 211, 240, 279, 319

Surname	folios
Cope	279
Copsey	300
Cordery	111, 121, 207, 212, 218, 286, 305
Corfe	105
Corkland	278
Corstorphon	278
Costelow	141, 326, 327
Cotton	198, 273
Cottrell	147, 271, 272
Cottrill	200
Couch	299
Coulsell	219, 220, 236
Coulson	252
Coulston	188
Cousins	186
Coveney	319
Covington	236
Cowdery	113, 216
Cowley	163
Cowpland	196
Cox	104, 108, 118, 266, 267, 277, 315, 335
Coxen	333
Craft	187
Craigh	331
Crandley	306
Craven	233
Crawley	213
Creed	145, 304
Crees	299
Creese	130
Cress	218
Crickett	19
Cripps	18, 19, 29, 74, 130, 169, 173, 248
Crisp	138
Crispin	104
Cristian (?)	107
Croft	21, 259, 260, 317
Crompton	328
Crook	135, 332
Croome	301
Cross	155, 256
Crouch	172, 175, 240
Crow	196, 274, 285, 308
Crowe	329
Crowhurst	164
Crowther	189
Crutchley	137
Cue	127
Cule	139
Cull	227
Cullis	280
Cullum	261, 262
Culver	131
Cumming	20

Surname	folios
Cunicke	262
Cunliffe	294
Cunningham	252
Curewood	121
Curner	113
Currall	249, 250
Currell	242, 286
Curtin	322
Curtis	211, 294, 315, 335
Curtiss	143
Curwood	187
Cussell	161
Cussen	229
Cuther	280
Cutler	278, 280
Cutting	32
Cuttis	15
Cuttrain	120
D'arcy	53
Dabourn	195
Daish	7
Dale	126, 302, 304
Daley	41
Dallas	106
Dalton	325
Damill	64
Dan Beslen	96
Daniel	95
Danks	14
Darrell	118
Dart	57, 286
Darvill	96
Dash	10, 66, 93
Davenport	196
Daves	330
Davey	139, 256, 289, 294, 308
David	110, 184
Davidge	285
Davidson	8, 102, 188
Davies	58, 63, 146, 161, 162, 195, 247
Davis	30, 42, 65, 83, 110, 156, 227, 235, 240, 242, 252, 257, 322, 334
Davison	158
Dawdes	53
Dawes	43
Dawn	263
Dawson	12
Day	165, 177, 262
De Boon (?)	53
De Friencry	280
De La Torr	35
De Vera	276

Surname	folios
Deady	166
Dean	48
Deane	133, 137, 143
Dearner	142, 144, 146, 149
Deaser	59
Deayton	47
Deedman	158
Deeks	280
Defau	251
Defoe	68
Dejerley (?)	208
Delany	20
Delarue	113
Dell	157
Dellas	52
Demarest	261
Deminiol	96
Dempsey	127
Dandy	144, 172
Denham	281
Denman	17, 22, 216, 297
Dennehy	127
Dennis	109, 297
Dennison	320
Denny	289
Dennys	185
Dent	147
Denyer	17, 166, 174, 218, 227, 287
Depeke (?)	146
Deriary	43
Derpard	198
Desbury	277
Devaney	53
Deverill	89
Dewar	331
Dewdney	31, 276
Dewfreville (?)	183
Dexter	325
Dicey	169, 303, 304, 307
Dickins	171
Dickson	72
Dilly	7, 326
Dinner	139
Dippie	294
Dixon	132, 195, 196, 202, 216, 249, 251, 279
Dobbs	60
Dobson	122, 326
Dodd	31, 95, 262
Doddrell	159
Dodge	34
Dodsworth	37
Dolamore	196
Dolh	194
Dolphin	281

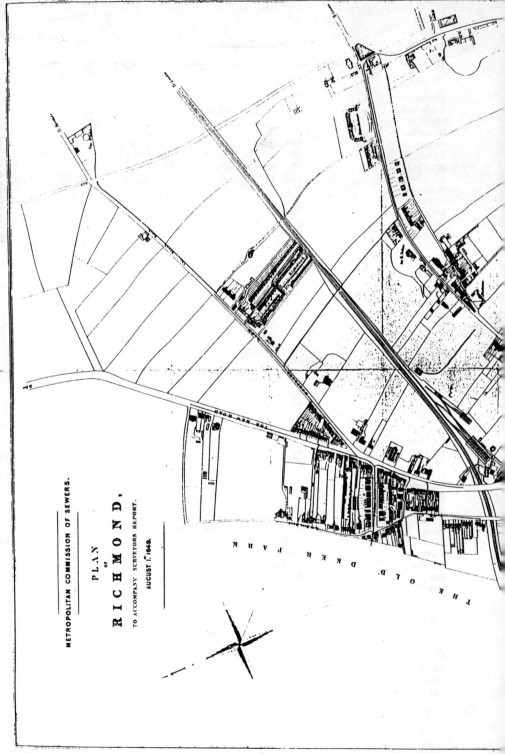

METROPOLITAN COMMISSION OF SEWERS.

PLAN
OF
RICHMOND,

TO ACCOMPANY SURVEYORS REPORT.

AUGUST 1. 1849.

THE OLD DEER PARK

Surname index

Surname	folios
Easley	213
Easton	62
Eaton	92, 250
Ebelland	108
Ebelling	325
Eddy	60
Ede	114, 276
Eden	86, 91, 116, 118, 130, 156, 166, 243
Edge	315
Edginton	176
Edmed	260
Edmonds	117
Edson	217
Edwards	61, 75, 87, 96, 113, 144, 147, 166, 171, 243, 259
Eggleston	41
Einlandt	53
Elderson	35
Eldridge	93, 235
Element	56
Elems	211
Eling	286
Elkington	7
Ellard	77, 101, 275
Ellett	126
Ellingham	226
Elliott	42, 43, 57, 65, 114, 136, 298
Ellis	5, 6, 36, 120, 184, 188, 194, 200, 217, 220, 263, 275, 319
Ellison	155
Ellsley	263
Ellwood	40
Elmes	193, 197, 237
Elsley	76, 325, 338
Elton	129
Emerton	168, 298
Emery	21, 47
Emmerson	216, 217, 249
Emmett	57, 183
Emmington	136
Enever	230
Equilbec	317
Errey	44
Esdaile	92
Ester	281
Etherington	47, 69, 96
Euson	187
Euston	38

Surname	folios
Evans	63, 105, 133, 158, 174, 199, 200, 236, 259, 282, 296
Evens	46, 143
Everall	262
Everett	133
Everton	168
Evison	185
Ewing	34
Ewmett	202
Exmouth	34
Eyles	232
Fabian	184
Faines	83
Fairbrother	86
Fairlie	327
Falvey	43
Fantham	118
Farbrother	176
Farebrother	103
Fario	127
Farlane	11
Farmer	88, 102
Farnsworth	59
Farr	334
Farrance	41
Farrand	236
Farrant	183
Farrar	38
Farrer	305
Farrow	146
Faulkner	90, 154, 190
Faunch	169, 322, 323, 329
Fearns	177
Fearon	92
Featherstone	280
Fellowes	321
Feltham	62
Fenn	212
Ferguson	319, 327
Fermor	60
Fern	137, 139
Ferndall	113
Fernie	338
Fialon	66
Fiddle	185
Fiddler	91
Fidy	159
Fiedler	330
Field	32, 47, 96, 142, 226, 318, 319, 335
Fields	135
Fiford	338
Figg	60, 256
Figget	253

Surname	folios
Figgin	336
Filkin	177
Filkins	328
Filtniss	90
Finch	40, 120, 121, 148, 227
Fincham	325
Findhope	168
Findlay	5
Findler (?)	161
Finlaison	58
Finnagan	53
Finney	39, 107
Firth	154
Fisher	30, 187, 191
Fitch	331
Fitt	20
Fitzgerald	8, 20, 53
Fitzpatrick	38-39, 159
Flack	7, 141, 234
Fland	143
Flask	212
Fleetwood	110
Fleming	201, 280
Flemmings	73
Fletcher	20, 56, 61, 115, 133, 164, 187, 189
Flight	198
Flina (?)	127
Flindh	336
Floater	329
Floris	296
Flower	285
Fludder	17
Foard	164
Fobles	337
Fod	157
Foley	134
Folkingham	57
Follett	60
Folley	198
Foot	278
Foothead	66-67
Forbes	5
Ford	40, 88, 166
Forder	185
Fording	141
Forey	304
Forssberg	329
Forster	134, 154
Forty	104, 140, 260
Foster	154, 173, 195, 208, 231, 262, 276
Fothergill	184
Foublanque	187
Fowkes	47
Fowler	230, 275, 335

Surname	folios
Fox	44, 58, 183, 323
Foy	157, 304
Fraenza	158
Frampton	260
Francis	36, 58, 77, 106, 118, 156, 257
Frand	57
Franklin	39, 106, 133, 134, 336
Franklyn	48, 249
Frawder	118
Fraxen (?)	315
Fray	303
Frazer	8, 93, 276
Freake	325
Freeman	82, 97
Freemantle	156
Freisen	315
French	34, 135, 176, 178, 209
Fresh	65
Frewin	40-41
Fribbins	35, 147, 211, 278
Fricker	110, 136
Frieth	53
Frilder (?)	186
Frim	298
Frimace	68
Frinder	119
Frith	237
Frock	116
Froes	53
Fromow	302
Fronblanque	45
Frost	28, 46, 121, 165, 250, 251, 252, 314
Fruin	15, 18
Fruine	32
Fry	31, 281
Fullbrook	308
Fuller	53, 84, 85, 114, 129, 164, 208, 217
Furze	136, 175
Gabille	177
Gabriel	32
Gadbale (?)	113
Gade	38
Gadger	64
Gadsby	68
Gaffray	10
Gaines	272
Gainfield	52
Gainton	157
Gale	333, 336
Galloway	194, 281
Gamble	297
Gander	69

Surname	folios
Garcia del Rio	53
Gardener	9, 175, 234, 299
Gardiner	19, 89, 281, 301
Gardner	9, 57, 69, 111
Garfield	177
Garland	112
Garratt	102
Garrett	32, 66, 297
Garrick	300
Garton	199
Gascoyne	62
Gate	16
Gates	236
Gathercole	197
Gatting	138
Gawne	29
Geden	37
Gee (?)	317
Gender	299
Genese	330
George	7, 139, 166, 301, 329
Gettings	10
Gibbins	33
Gibbons	248, 293
Gibbs	33
Gibson	94, 108, 286
Gifford	156, 314
Gilbert	36, 53, 97, 104, 141, 329
Gilder	253
Giles	184, 193, 200, 201, 212, 262
Gilgrass	253
Gilham	216
Gillard	324
Gillett	275
Gilman	83
Gimingham	301
Gingele	134
Gittings	10
Gladman	257
Glass	105
Glazier	138
Gloss	217
Glover	77, 93, 94, 118, 278
Godard	72
Goddard	71, 160, 194, 230
Godfrey	69, 75, 199, 315
Godwin	70, 114
Goff	28
Golard	280
Goldfinch	232, 233
Goldsby	38
Good	64
Goodale	64
Goodall	157, 195, 294

Surname	folios
Goodchild	256
Goode	186
Gooderham	133
Goodes	187
Goodhall	264
Gooding	10, 111, 163
Goodman	127, 129, 137, 162, 218
Goodridge	111, 144
Goodrow	6
Goodwin	31, 45, 64, 109, 198, 327
Goran (?)	157
Gordon	147, 184
Gore	67, 217
Goreing	219
Gormbridge	157
Gosden	316
Gosling	174, 182, 183, 232
Gouldsmith	68
Gover	241
Govett	325
Govier	318
Gowar	28
Gowis (?)	107
Grace	57, 189
Graham	276
Granger	236, 281
Grant	27, 35, 318
Grantham	318
Grarhalgh (?)	233
Grates	76
Gratton	131
Gratwick	9, 92
Graut	21
Gray	45, 187, 242, 258, 273, 278, 332
Graydon	281
Grayland	113
Greatrex	289
Green	61, 66, 69, 94, 176, 217, 234
Greenaway	13, 167
Greene	66, 93
Greener	228
Greenfield	142
Greenham	35
Greenhead	333
Greenland	110
Greenlaw	326
Greenway	303
Greenwood	15, 234
Gregory	21, 44-45, 328
Grenville	301
Grey	117
Gridler	161
Gridley	39, 208
Grieve	8

Surname	folios
Hanford	62
Hanington	64
Hanna	57
Hannay	326
Hannemann	336
Hanniford	202
Hannon	324
Hanon	281
Hanratty	127
Hansard	155, 175
Hanson	30
Harbird	306
Hardcastle	192
Harden	87
Harding	84, 118, 140, 183, 273, 317
Hare	34, 45
Harfield	14
Hargrave	315
Harley	87
Harman	119, 120, 121
Harmer	57
Harmes	63
Harper	6, 22, 33, 47, 48, 316, 317
Harridge	93
Harrington	175
Harris	28, 43, 66, 114, 155, 161, 166, 174, 198, 213, 229, 239, 248, 289, 299, 307, 330, 334, 338
Harrison	14, 35, 64, 86, 213, 237, 238, 239, 284, 332
Harrod	337
Harsell	85
Hart	33, 44, 92, 177, 230, 316, 338
Harthman	84
Hartlebury	33, 40, 71, 165, 191, 215, 216, 299
Harvey	63, 120, 155, 194
Harward	172, 264
Hassall	103
Hassell	195
Hatch	331
Hatfield	63, 118
Hatton	66
Hauchet	294
Hawes	328, 333
Hawkes	36, 37, 45, 106
Hawkins	66, 322
Hawks	61
Hawley	304
Hawthorn	200, 277
Haydon	69
Hayhoe	296, 297
Haynes	82, 302, 335, 336
Haysman	12
Hayter	114, 130
Hayward	136
Haywood	189

Surname	folios
Hazlewood	263
Head	159
Headington	83, 262
Heakes	262
Heales	286
Healey	145
Hearn	104, 210
Hearson	300
Heasford	316
Heath	134, 153, 189, 202
Heathen	295
Heather	318
Hebden	102, 294
Hedger	172
Hedges	110, 111, 135, 287, 302, 337
Heely	114
Helps	336
Hempsted	301
Henderson	331
Hendery	296
Hendet	329
Henesey	53
Henneguin	154
Henry	52, 92, 104
Hepper	113
Herbert	5, 293
Herdsfield	294
Heritage	39
Herman	12
Hermon	36
Herod	146
Herring	33
Herring	193, 207
Herris	107
Hervey	170a
Hesketh	34
Hester	110
Heubergen	90
Hewah	184
Hewer	317
Hewitt	133, 226, 247, 295
Hewkins	56
Hewsoll	183
Heyhoe	13
Heyrick	38
Heywood	111
Hickox	46
Higgins	40, 318, 327
Higgs	12, 87, 185, 238
Highmore	91
Highs	208
Higley	39
Hilder	256
Hilditch	87

Surname	folios
Hile	132, 133
Hill	41, 52, 59, 63, 89, 117, 163, 183, 197, 200, 201, 231, 316
Hillier	211, 273, 313
Hillman	112
Hills	88, 308
Hillyer	186
Hilman	234
Hilton	92
Hinde	327
Hines	320
Hinstone	57
Hinton	183
Hinwood	41, 174
Hipping (?)	248
Hirons	279
Hiscock	313, 326, 330
Hisloke	27
Hitch	137
Hitchcock	133, 208, 228, 240, 262, 308
Hitchin	63
Hoad	161
Hoalston	332
Hobday	285
Hobson	325, 326
Hockley	304, 305, 306
Hodges	175
Hodgkinson	276
Hodgson	96, 101, 132, 158
Hogg	34, 71, 285, 287
Holden	211, 214, 217
Holder	77
Holding	248
Holdstock	127
Holl	282
Holland	201
Holley	159, 201, 220, 252, 279
Holloway	26, 56, 143, 288
Holly	183
Holman	104
Holmes	34, 66, 115, 153, 211
Holt	34, 144, 303
Honor	212
Hood	11
Hoodless	58
Hoogson	40
Hook	195
Hooper	162, 184, 280
Hooperton	109
Hope	176, 207, 299, 300
Hoper	27
Hopkins	112
Hopperman	279
Hopping	248

Surname	folios
Hopstroff	137
Hopwood	157, 226
Hormlerton (?)	127
Horn	294
Hornabrook	284
Horne	108
Horton	10, 161
Hosbar	306
Hosier	64, 130
Hosking	63
Hoskins	27, 30, 64, 298
Hossock	157
Hosswood	64
Houghton	284
Houliston	332
Hounslow	231
House	42, 44
Hove	9
Howard	8, 63, 70, 72, 112, 120, 157, 277, 306, 307
Howcroft	198
Howe	5, 217, 318, 319
Howel	337
Howell	298
Howells	45
Howes	83
Howey	281
Howill	46
Howlett	89
Howlings	279
Hudson	38, 182, 266, 294, 316
Huggett	144
Huggins	135, 282
Hugh	114
Hughes	7, 13, 129, 192, 332
Hukin	202
Humby	183
Hume	175, 284
Humphrey	28
Humphreys	38, 62, 169, 174, 189, 251, 254, 322, 323, 326
Humphries	33, 192
Hunt	111, 128, 146, 175, 254, 262, 273, 293
Hunter	235
Huntsman	45
Hurbart	284
Hurnod (?)	239
Hurt	19, 106
Hurtshore	114
Hussey	40
Hutchins	62, 120, 146, 163, 227, 252, 283
Hutchinson	328, 331
Hutson	187, 320
Hutt	37, 239, 240
Hyams	330
Hyatt	227

Surname	folios
Jones	322
Jordan	139
Joseph	329, 330
Joy	197
Joyce	167
Judge	127
Juett	69
Jugwood (?)	19
Jukes	289
Julius	88, 89, 186
Jutt	33
Jux	220
Keaney	128
Keay	60
Keegan	319
Keen	256, 317
Keene	35, 40, 43, 157
Keith	195
Kelly	106
Kelsall	5
Kelsey	307
Kemble	333, 338
Kemp	75, 92, 285
Kendon	298
Kendrick	155, 159
Kensett	276
Kent	241 , 250, 254
Kern	7
Kerriston	43
Kershaw	163, 164
Kert	186
Ketteridge	17
Kew	275
Key	30, 317
Kidd	284
Kidman	12
Kidner	74
Kilbey	276
Kilby	30
Kilgore	140
Kilgour	253, 256, 257
Killett	37
Killingsby	61
Kine	34
King	32-33, 38, 87, 171, 174, 183, 192, 231, 256, 259, 266, 282, 287, 315, 321, 332, 333
Kingshott	199
Kingsland	165
Kingston	183, 211
Kinilin (?)	198
Kirbey	44
Kirby	29, 30, 40, 44, 198, 219, 221, 236, 247, 327, 332

Surname	folios
Kirkhouse	199
Kirkman	60, 163
Kitley	334
Kitson	248
Knesabeck	315
Knight	18, 45, 113, 326
Knowles	189
Korkman	60
La Terrine	95
Lacey	38, 156, 304
Lack	44
Lacy	31, 182
Ladlice	301
Lafitte	127
Laidler	36
Laining	228
Laker	130
Lamb	7, 57, 280
Lambert	7, 55, 102
Lamer	293
Laming	160
Lancaster	209, 241
Lane	32, 135, 275, 335
Langford	254, 265, 323
Langham	92
Langley	44, 149
Langridge	64, 148, 161, 252, 260, 276
Langston	138, 162, 191, 237, 252, 258
Langstone	218
Langton	62
Lanham	141
Larcomb	35
Lark	45, 155
Larkin	146
Larkman	307
Larner	293
Lascelles	232
Lavington	28
Lawrence	56, 93, 135, 153, 189, 295, 299
Lawson	28
Layton	319
Le Blond	282
Lea	320
Leach	11
Leadbitter	54
Leathren (?)	196
Leawham	19
Leck	90, 254, 257, 263
Leckie	127
Leclerc	127
Ledder	128
Ledge	326
Ledger	17-18, 234, 322, 324

Surname	folios
Lee	41-42, 67, 95, 168, 185, 299, 330
Lees	183, 321
Leigh	332
Lemon	257
Leon	330
Lesiter	286
Leslie	177
Letchford	249
Levi	133, 329
Levin	213, 250
Lewen	20
Lewes	335
Lewis	13-14, 20, 27, 64, 65, 68, 106, 109, 115, 145, 167, 174, 254, 298, 317, 324
Liddeard	133
Liddiard	327
Liddy	116
Light	30-31, 295
Lillence	289
Lillford	146
Lilly	6
Lilywhite	324
Linden	328
Lindenburg	34
Lindsay	65, 212
Lindsey	118
Line	11, 34
Lineker	158
Lines	10, 191
Lipscombe	103
List	294
Lister	56
Litchfield	156
Littel	187
Litten	208
Little	10,18, 238
Littlefield	141
Littlejohn	164
Littleton	7
Littlewood	34, 195
Littleworth	302
Livers (?)	117
Lloyd	36, 140, 163, 197, 210, 334
Loane	280
Loaving	165
Lock	21
Lockyer	167
Locock	86
Lodden	239
Loftus	194
Logan	236
Loisel	138
Lomas	110
London	88, 148

Surname	folios
Long	17, 18, 19, 32, 41, 54, 56, 62, 67, 69, 118, 132, 136, 164, 202, 215, 218, 220, 226, 266, 279, 301
Longhurst	107, 272
Longman	13
Loose	62
Lord	75
Loscam (?)	92
Loud	188
Loudon	140
Love	208
Lovegrove	30
Lovelace	319
Lovell	47
Lovelock	58, 301
Lovett	9, 13, 88
Low	316
Lowe	147, 184, 191, 192, 247, 264, 280
Lowin	219
Lowther	198
Loxbey	83
Loxley	95
Loyd	192, 330
Luard	88
Lubbock	230
Lucas	6, 43, 175, 200, 276
Luce	319
Luckett	29
Luff	96, 199, 216, 299, 319, 328, 329, 335
Luker	40, 132, 271
Lurman	321
Lusguiorny (?)	57
Luxton	234
Lyde	183
Lyford	195
Lynch	54
Lyne	39
Lyney	38
Lyons	48
Lysaght	280
Loisel	138
Lomas	110
London	88, 148
Long	17, 18, 19, 32, 41, 54, 56, 62, 67, 69, 118, 132, 136, 164, 202, 215, 218, 220, 226, 266, 279, 301
Longhurst	107, 272
Longman	13
Loose	62
Lord	75
Loscam (?)	92
Loud	188
Loudon	140
Love	208

Surname	folios
Lovegrove	30
Lovelace	319
Lovell	47
Lovelock	58, 301
Lovett	9, 13, 88
Low	316
Lowe	147, 184, 191, 192, 247, 264, 280
Lowin	219
Lowther	198
Loxbey	83
Loxley	95
Loyd	192, 330
Luard	88
Lubbock	230
Lucas	6, 43, 175, 200, 276
Luce	319
Luckett	29
Luff	96, 199, 216, 299, 319, 328, 329, 335
Luker	40, 132, 271
Lurman	321
Lusguiorny (?)	57
Luxton	234
Lyde	183
Lyford	195
Lynch	54
Lyne	39
Lyney	38
Lyons	48
Lysaght	280
MacAuliff	52
MacAuliffe	54
MacBean	239
MacCardy	128
MacCreay	202
MacDonald	54, 59, 74, 128
MacDonnell	183
Macey	208
MacGair	94
MacGillvray	5
MacGlashen	34
MacGrigor	65
MacIntosh	77
Mack	118
Mackay	122, 198, 253
Mackenna	90
MacKenzie	8, 157, 184
MacKinney	6, 303, 305
MacKinnie	84
Macklin	5
MacLachlan	230
MacNab	301
MacNair	156, 201, 202
MacPherson	64

Surname	folios
Mauhal	43
Maurice	316
Mausbridge	289
Mausele	133
Mawsan	120
Maxwell	172
May	217, 239, 281
Mayen (?)	330
Mayhead	198, 203
Mayhew	93, 195
Mayne	134
Mayo	90
Mead	58, 111
Meadford	68
Meadows	170a, 295
Meads	316
Meeson	296
Meggatt	147
Meighan	331
Mekrew	32
Mellish	65, 131, 155, 176, 272, 273
Menhennet	149
Menzies	91, 103
Mercer	102, 256, 275
Merredith	131
Merreditt	102
Merrill	66, 105
Merring	93
Merritt	59
Messenger	27, 72, 286, 287
Messum	70, 72, 91, 215
Metcalf	60
Mews	138
Meymott	93
Miale	137
Michaels	57
Middleship	194, 316
Middleton	48, 233
Middlewich	184
Milan	259
Milan	133
Miles	19, 92, 109, 259
Mill	44
Millar	63, 195
Millard	132
Miller	9, 52, 62, 65, 134, 184, 226, 236, 274, 278
Milliken	190
Milliner	148
Mills	5, 63, 94, 212, 232, 237, 308, 329
Milman	326
Milne	32
Milner	137
Milson	280
Milstead	46

Surname	folios
Minter	37
Missin	239
Mitchele	113
Moates	6
Moffat	302
Moher	307
Moisey	136
Mole	193
Molesworth	185
Monasson	298
Monday	239, 327
Moody	149, 236, 288
Moore	66, 109, 113, 298, 326
Moosey	168
Mordaunt	21
Moreland	238
Morgan	333
Moris	75
Morley	127, 128, 178
Morrell	136
Morris	8, 10, 32, 58, 85, 90, 137, 187, 210, 219, 261, 320
Morrison	314
Morse	69
Morshead	36
Mortimer	138
Morton	5, 30, 275
Moscrop	92
Mosely	219, 329, 330
Moses	330
Moss	59, 129, 175, 214, 229, 234, 235
Moule	56
Mousey	107
Mowbray	140
Moyan	6
Moyles	67
Muff	146
Muggridge	321
Mullinger	200
Mullins	182
Mumford	253
Muncesday	157
Munro	274, 322
Muredew	82
Murphy	193, 316
Murray	44, 58, 121, 122, 266
Murrell	108
Murrey	13
Murrows	41
Mussell	73
Myers	54, 330
Myring	43

Surname	folios
Nairne	27
Naish	168, 172, 258, 298
Nalder	220
Napier	104
Narney	40
Nash	117, 147, 153, 163, 258, 276, 287, 294
Neach	155
Neal	12, 17, 263
Neale	29, 40, 195
Neil	170a, 297
Neill	277
Nelhaines	45
Nelham	169
Nelhams	90, 91, 249, 257
Nethersole	102
Netherwood	67
Nettlefold	19
Neumegen	329
Nevill	28, 36, 141, 198, 325
New	75, 77, 121, 137, 279, 284, 285
Newby	169
Newell	84
Newens	108
Newlan	243
Newman	39, 65, 109, 112, 167, 194, 233, 325
Newsom	155
Newton	107, 132, 188
Nicholls	111, 200, 217, 218, 298, 327
Nicholson	20, 108, 155, 195
Nicklin	94
Nightingale	316
Nigrah	147
Nisbridge	113
Niven	316
Noble	266
Nokes	27
Nolan	157
Nolari	35
Nolgrove	192
Noller	41
Norbury	20, 66
Norman	34, 76, 157, 233, 261, 301
Normond	273
Norris	28, 46, 198, 296
Northan	86
Norton	43, 314
Norville	114
Nowlan	334
Noyce	276
Nulty	53
Nunan	229
Nunn	307
Nunns	198

Surname	folios
Pavely	112
Pavier	295, 296
Payne	301
Paynter	57
Peachey	295
Peacock	155, 176
Pearce	148, 160, 162, 334
Pearmund	237, 263
Pearse	61
Pearson	295
Peart	201
Peats	14
Peck	6
Peek	149, 170a, 230, 231
Peile	301
Peirce	207, 216
Peiyelley	185
Pelling	110
Pellitill	54
Pemberton	198
Penfold	277, 286, 325
Penn	30, 332
Pennington	273
Penny	57, 170
Penston	47, 117
Pentelow	133
Pentridge	319
Pepper	155, 299
Pepperell	37
Percival	249
Perdo	280
Perkins	21, 74, 105
Perrett	94, 112
Perrott	164
Perry	211, 220, 225
Persse	289
Pescott	241
Pescud	216, 240
Pesnell	233
Peters	55, 112, 118, 120, 200, 300
Peterson	57
Pethebridge	164
Petley	236
Pettit	11
Petty	316
Pfender	275
Phead	182
Phebey	148
Pheby	59, 164
Phelan	177
Philips	57, 184
Phillips	60, 62, 64, 68
Phillipson	200
Phipps	190

Surname	folios
Pourney	12
Povey	257
Powe	110
Powell	16, 91, 196, 217, 280, 288
Power	85
Powles	102
Poyser	58
Poyson	185
Pratt	7, 11, 46, 138
Prause	133
Pressley	300
Pretious	317
Prewell	226
Price	17, 93, 103, 138, 141, 142, 154, 177, 197, 239, 242, 247, 278, 294
Priestley	120, 322
Prince	92
Pring	320
Prior	153, 199, 284, 314
Pritchard	13
Pritchett	277
Prole	62, 140
Prosser	62, 208
Pryor	273
Pugh	119
Puison (?)	142
Pullen	7, 147, 263, 272
Pulleyne	92
Pullin	126
Pullinger	140
Pulman	326, 328
Pummell	109
Purdey	171
Putman	140
Puzey	274
Pyne	54
Pyther	177
Quar	92
Quarterman	128
Queensberry	10
Quevillant	322
Quick	20-21
Quill	54
Quin	191
Quinlain	115
Quintin	147
Quick	20-21
Quill	54
Quin	191
Quinlain	115
Quintin	147

Surname	folios
Racklass	32
Radford	31, 237, 263
Rae	16
Raffey	168
Raggett	172
Rainbow	121
Raine	328
Raith	161
Ramage	93
Ramsay	12, 85
Ramsey	161, 168
Ramton	157
Randall	59
Ranson	31
Rapley	77, 325
Rapom	197
Ratcliff	129
Ratford	130
Rattan	54
Ravenshaw	161
Rawlings	6, 254
Rayley	165
Raymond	321
Razor	247
Rea	282
Read	60, 135, 184, 243, 282, 324
Reading	85, 158, 214
Reardon	102, 197, 225
Reay	274
Reddin	127
Redfern	12
Redford	109
Redmass	73
Redsell	300
Reed	10, 112, 147, 209, 271
Reeds	133
Reeve	133, 184, 230
Reeves	72, 337
Regnart	247
Reid	104
Reily	115
Reive	136
Reldon	225
Relph (?)	64
Remnant	261, 267
Renard	294
Renlidge	65
Rennett	77
Rennie	6
Renny	7
Renton	47
Reynell	182
Reynolds	8, 33, 35, 92, 265
Reyshew	323

Surname	folios
Rhodes	14, 37
Rice	19, 38, 40, 157, 317
Richard	277
Richards	36, 37, 88, 319
Richardson	5, 77, 84, 142, 185, 192, 208, 210, 305
Rickford	95
Rickman	146
Riddell	154
Ridden	282
Rider	42
Ridge	10
Ried	189
Rigby	76, 307, 324, 325
Rigge	317
Riley	302, 336
Rinfield	238
Ring	331
Ringer	308
Ripley	281
Rising	138
Rivar (?)	102
Rivett	54
Roach	83, 264
Roberts	5, 16, 44, 45, 90, 115, 155, 185, 188, 232, 276, 277, 300, 315
Robertson	20, 66, 86, 113, 130, 142, 194
Robey	61
Robins	128, 251
Robinson	35, 46, 116, 134, 164, 194, 230, 237, 260, 279, 323
Robottom	74
Robson	276, 336
Rochester	147
Rockwell	122
Roden	276
Roebuck	28
Rogers	12, 36, 148, 235, 315
Rokins	171
Rolf	276
Rolfe	20
Rolls	154
Roper	334
Rosam	91
Rose	87, 234, 294
Ross	18, 88, 240
Rossiter	87
Roth	5
Rotton	132
Rouse	101
Routeledge	174
Rowe	128
Rowland	46, 54, 61, 332
Rowles	228

Surname	folios
Roy	184
Rudd	136, 137
Rudman	46
Rummings	155
Rusell	40
Rushton	314
Russell	104, 107, 111, 121, 144, 208, 209, 253, 254, 276, 331
Ruth	195
Rutherford	157
Rutland	30
Rutter	143, 316, 320
Ryall	88
Ryan	158, 266
Ryder	33, 111
Rye	250
Ryland	37
Sack	126
Saddington	318
Safewell	131
Saking	73
Sale	41, 47
Salmon	96
Salter	58, 64
Salteri	127
Salvage	46
Samples	333
Sampson	330
Samson	329
Samuel	62, 330
Sandens	308, 309
Sanders	5, 97, 131, 162, 254, 296
Sandey	9
Sandison	198
Sanford	190
Sankey	239
Sargent	247
Sarner	277
Satchill	41
Saunders	39, 59, 69, 120, 196, 233, 254, 288, 318
Savell	211
Savill	32
Sawer	337
Saws	37
Sawyer	36, 169
Scarville	40
Schaddick	325
Scheer	325
Schofield	233
Schriner	275
Scoles	128
Scophard	29
Score	131, 272

Surname	folios
Scotford	39, 157, 163
Scott	13, 18-19, 44, 45, 67, 157, 165, 196, 220, 227, 273, 285
Scully	108
Sculstrop	134
Seale	35
Sealey	140
Sealy	277
Seares	314
Searle	162, 307
Seaton	64, 195
Seaward	314
Sec	56
Sedgwick	142, 143
Sedgworth	114
Seely	59
Segwick	18
Selden	114, 115
Selle	95, 323
Sells	321
Selviton (?)	13
Selwyn	164, 230
Sessions	315
Setford	142
Settree	140
Sewter	72
Seymour	199
Shackell	132
Shadd	121
Shadwell	130, 185, 279, 288, 303, 305
Shaftesbury	197
Shale	258
Shallard	184
Shanks	185
Shann	69
Sharp	13, 20, 47, 61, 121, 331
Sharpe	87, 129, 143, 295
Sharples	261
Shater	14
Shaw	5, 45, 135, 185, 317, 327
Shaylor	10
Shead	284
Shear	43
Shears	202
Sheath	85
Sheene (?)	116
Sheffield	317
Shelton	57
Shepherd	249, 315, 333
Sheppard	88
Sheridan	35, 47
Shermen	158
Sherratt	30
Sherriff	157

Surname	folios
Sherrin	196, 265
Shettle	296
Sheward	326
Shields	276
Shiffier	59
Shilton	35
Shingleton	248, 249, 258, 259, 303, 306
Shinners	257
Shirreff	281
Shoobrook	28
Shopland	163
Shore	118, 141, 170, 219, 236, 303, 333
Short	156
Shorter	167
Shrimpton	108
Shuttlewood	60
Shuttleworth	272
Sibley	5
Sidney	329
Silver	218
Silverwood	197
Silvester	172
Simmonds	35, 108, 157
Simmons	128
Simms	5, 30
Simpkins	61
Simpson	89, 324
Sims	129, 142, 207, 242, 285, 299
Singleton	46, 85, 90, 162, 173, 230, 263, 278, 327
Sivaby	227
Sketchley	113
Skillon	35
Skinner	19, 95, 108
Slack	21, 199
Slade	174, 260
Slammers	271
Slater	30, 73
Slaughter	176
Slee	106
Sleeman	96
Slevin	21
Slevise	67
Slight	174
Sloly	183
Sloman	330
Slowman	330
Sludley (?)	199
Smallman	177
Smallpiece	46
Smart	39, 95, 176, 195
Smastley	88
Smith	12, 21, 29, 31, 32, 33, 34, 38, 54, 57, 59, 62, 63, 64, 65, 66, 74, 84, 89, 90, 91, 92, 94, 96, 102, 103, 108, 113, 118, 119, 129, 131, 133, 136,

Surname	folios
Smith	148, 155, 157, 158, 163, 176, 177, 185, 187, 194, 195, 196, 202, 212, 213, 213, 240, 241, 253, 257, 274, 275, 277, 278, 282, 288, 295, 296, 297, 299, 301, 303, 308, 316, 317, 323, 325, 333, 336
Smyth	8, 54
Snelgrove	43
Snell	40, 48, 214
Snelling	8, 59, 315
Soden	184, 209
Sole	63
Solomon	329, 330
Sookie	294
Soulsby	87
Sousdale	131
Souter	7
South	61, 313
Southin	209, 210
Sovrell	144
Sowter	314, 330
Spalding	40, 61
Sparks	193
Sparshott	183
Spearing	143
Speiling	5
Spence	109
Spencer	110, 174, 231
Spendlove	13
Spicer	60
Spiers	120, 183
Spory (?)	197
Spreadborough	103
Springall	31
Springett	210
Square	33
St Albyn	200
St John	127, 293
Stable	300, 301
Stacey	108, 111, 112, 138, 144, 189, 275, 307
Stafford	21
Stagg	315
Staley	114
Stamford	238
Stamp	271
Stanbury	138
Standers	212
Stanfield	54, 129
Stanford	84, 185, 188, 190
Stanley	85, 314
Staples	116, 283
Stapleton	65, 232
Stapley	170a, 189, 229, 238, 266
Start	5
Stavely	273
Stayne	62

Surname	folios
Taco	54
Taghill	172, 173
Taite	20
Talbot	29, 54
Tame	135
Tanner	101, 154
Tanton	254
Taplin	36, 101, 337
Tarleton	321
Tarr	5
Tarrant	20
Tasker	34, 93, 134, 309
Tate	10
Tayler	255, 256
Taylor	7, 18, 19, 21, 31, 37, 39, 47, 61, 63, 64, 65, 97, 102, 117, 126, 140, 142, 174, 185, 190, 197, 201, 209, 211, 213, 253, 259, 262, 263, 264, 293, 295, 303, 313, 315, 318, 321, 328, 333
Teale	61
Teatman	142
Tebbet	27
Tebbett	154
Tebbit	155
Tedbury	140
Tegnell	41
Temple	241
Templeton	316
Terry	57, 120
Tewan	27
Thalen	84
Thatcher	250, 307
Thead	303
Therry	307
Theusiac (?)	65
Thomas	15, 29, 43, 44, 103, 115, 175, 207
Thompson	63, 70, 87, 104, 106, 194, 293, 299, 332, 334
Thomson	57, 106, 158
Thornett	274
Thornhill	319
Thornton	34, 177, 191, 282, 326
Thorpe	195
Thuillier	88
Thwates	195
Tibballs	213
Tickner	169
Tidbury	140, 171
Tidy	86, 109
Tilbury	73
Tiller	242
Tilley	156
Tillin	211
Timms	328
Timpson	227
Tipping	161

Surname	folios
Ward	63, 102, 118, 167, 183, 231, 319, 321, 327
Warden	7, 230
Wardle	32
Ware	178
Wareham	323
Warkwick (?)	37
Warne	62, 316
Warner	31, 160, 207
Warr	21, 280
Warren	7, 40, 115, 133, 147, 160, 167, 256
Waterhouse •	106
Waterman	140, 158, 167
Watford	17
Watkins	42, 162, 170, 218, 226, 304, 327
Watson	32, 153, 241, 251, 297, 315
Watton	66
Watts	58, 59, 104, 126, 130, 145, 198, 295
Wayland	19, 112, 128, 130, 272, 274
Waymouh (?)	197
Weascall	65
Weaver	31, 316, 337
Webb	7, 11, 29, 86, 95, 105, 106, 111, 113, 148, 167, 241, 263, 288
Webster	5, 29, 39, 54, 61, 65, 219
Wedding	241
Wedgbury	315
Weedon	157, 210
Weigh	197
Weighton	187
Welch	178, 208, 235, 299, 320
Welland	165
Weller	20, 325
Wells	86, 47, 154, 161, 164, 185, 251, 256, 280, 283, 302, 330
Welsh	94, 146, 327
Wenring	140
Wescoth	35
West	96, 163, 164, 175, 187, 197, 208, 241, 285
Westbrook	184, 301
Westcott	6
Westfold	289
Weston	147, 153, 202, 203, 211, 217, 284, 307
Westwood	145, 153
Weth	190
Wetherall	89
Wetton	301
Whale	89
Whar	86
Whatman	295
Whatmore	337
Whaymore	146
Wheatley	41, 162, 296
Wheeler	40, 70, 77, 87, 109, 110, 111, 114, 185, 208, 240, 242, 286, 305

Surname	folios
Whetstone	315
Whilton	139
Whipple	213
Whitbread	239
White	8, 12, 38, 92, 103, 104, 105, 107, 118, 144, 155, 176, 201, 274, 296, 327, 335, 336, 338
Whitehead	145, 166, 167, 184
Whitehorn	48
Whitehouse	183
Whiteland	62, 69, 145, 236, 303
Whitely	156
Whitfield	165, 225, 226, 247, 293
Whitland	38, 165
Whitmore	10
Whitten	186, 219
Whitton	242
Whyte	320
Wickey	31
Wicks	236
Widgley	64
Wiggins	295
Wigton (?)	21
Wild	137, 186, 319, 333
Wilder	198
Wilkes	260
Wilkins	202, 213
Wilkinson	61, 185
Willard	65
Willbred	44
Willcox	164
Willey	7
Williams	13, 37, 41, 47, 57, 64, 78, 88, 118, 139, 144, 167, 168, 173, 187, 195, 238, 241, 264, 272, 281, 315, 316, 329, 335, 338
Williamson	39, 333
Willim	299
Willis	40, 160, 177, 196, 315, 318, 327
Willman	164
Willmar (?)	30
Willmer	141
Willow	6, 9
Wills	86
Willson	75
Wilmott	299
Wilson	12, 61, 106, 115, 159, 164, 174, 192, 239, 308, 317, 318, 322
Wilton	14, 282
Wiltshire	255
Winacke (?)	8
Winall	107, 254
Winch	9, 12, 14
Winder	58
Windibank	207
Winfield	91, 101